The Psychology of Children's Art

The Psychology of Children's Art

by Rhoda Kellogg with Scott O'Dell

a psychology today book

CRM-Random House Publication
Published by CRM Inc.
Distributed by Random House

About the Authors

Rhoda Kellogg, internationally known authority on children's art, has spent the last 20 years collecting, analyzing, and interpreting more than 1,000,000 paintings and drawings made by children from the United States and 30 other countries.

As a leading nursery-school educator, Rhoda Kellogg has been in an enviable position to collect children's art. In 1928, she organized San Francisco's first nursery school and during World War II she was the director of 11 California nursery schools. Now she is the director of the Phoebe A. Hearst Preschool Learning Center and of the Golden Gate Kindergarten Association in San Francisco.

A graduate of the University of Minnesota in 1920, Rhoda Kellogg holds a Master's Degree in nursery-school education from Columbia University. She is the author of five books: *Analyzing Children's Art, What Children Scribble and Why, The How of Successful Finger Painting, Nursery School Guide,* and *Babies Need Fathers, Too.*

The Psychology of Children's Art is the first *Psychology Today* book. It grew out of the lead article in the charter issue of PSYCHOLOGY TODAY, the new monthly magazine about psychology, society, and the human condition.

Scott O'Dell, winner of the 1961 John Newberry Medal for the modern classic, *Island of the Blue Dolphins,* joined forces with Rhoda Kellogg to make *The Psychology of Children's Art* as beautiful to read as it is to look at. Widely known and loved by the children of the world *(Island of the Blue Dolphins* has been translated into 15 languages), Scott O'Dell during the past two years has talked to some 100,000 United States schoolchildren in his attempts to stimulate their interest in reading.

Scott O'Dell was born in Los Angeles and attended Occidental College and Stanford University. He has been a newspaperman, a magazine editor, and is the author of seven books, including *The King's Fifth* and *The Black Pearl.*

He has received the following awards for his writing:
John Newberry Medal
William Allen White Award
Hans Christian Andersen Award of Merit
Southern California Council on Children's Literature Award
German Juvenile Book Council International Award
Rupert Hughes Award
Hawaii State Nene Award

Contents

1 | The Search

Through the years adventurous men and women have searched the hills and valleys and mountains of the earth, seeking forms of life that existed once when our world was very young.

The search has been long and usually fruitless. Yet a day of good fortune did come when in the deeps of the earth something secret was found. To the untrained eye, it would have seemed little more than a pattern in the ancient dust. But to the knowing it was the remains of a creature that had lived and died in a land where reptiles had legs and ferns grew as tall as trees, a country we can scarcely imagine. Carefully put together these bare bones formed the skeleton of a brontosaur, a pterodactyl, or perhaps a horned dinosaur. This was a beginning, and still the search goes on.

And so it was with the pictures in this book. They are the findings of a search that has lasted now for more than twenty

This pensive sunflower had its origin in a painting of the sun. One of its elongated rays forms the stem.

With the flat of his hand, a three-year-old boy created this extraordinary finger painting, whose ruby center glows with a deep and mysterious fire.

years among the schools of the world, and wherever children are given paper and pencils and crayons. In a true sense these works of art are the bare bones of a great skeleton.

When the remnants of the first dinosaur were found, no one knew how or if they would fit together. Nor how it would look once the bones were assembled. Nor did the fabulous creature have a name, for it was something new to the eyes of man. The preparation of this book offered a challenge equally as great, yet different.

In the first place, there were only a few dozen dinosaur bones to sort out and arrange. But the pieces of children's art at hand numbered more than a million, half of them drawn by children below the age of six and the rest by those in grade school. Secondly, the bones were found in a rough pattern which suggested form and size, the original beast itself. But the millions of pieces of art at first suggested nothing, save the fact of a vast creative outpouring.

This creative thrust, however, was in itself a clue. It showed upon study that the artistic impulse is universal, as strong among the children of Korea or Spain or Siam as it is among the children of the Americas. Moreover, it pointed the way to the exciting discovery that all children everywhere draw the same things in the same way at the same age. For example, a child living in the city of Pusan, Korea, and a child of Amarillo, Texas, draw houses that look alike. Each makes a square to form the walls, a smaller square to show a window, an elongated square for the chimney, a curly scribble to indicate smoke. Indeed, the houses are so much alike that the national origin of the young artists might well be the same. So strong is the creative impulse among the young that this universality holds true for thirty houses drawn by thirty

The most dramatic aspect of this scribbling was achieved when the child accidentally used a near-perfect combination of color and balance. Were the colors reversed — yellow substituted for purple and purple for yellow — the painting would lose its power.

different children in thirty different countries.

In the natural course of learning to draw, from their very first lines to their later pictorial pieces, all children pass through the same stages of development. These stages may vary from child to child, or overlap like waves in the sea.

At about the age of two every child begins to scribble. He scribbles on paper, if it is given to him, on fences, on fresh concrete, or in the sand with his toes. To the adult, scribbling may seem senseless, but to the child it is as natural as eating a cookie; it is a natural thing to do with fingers and toes—and it is meaningful.

When he begins to scribble, even upon the vagrant air, the child already has a primitive sense of figure-ground relationships. His scribbles do not fall at random on whatever space he is using. Instead they are placed in definite patterns—in the left half, the right half, or even in the center. Seventeen such placement patterns have been recognized and identified. Once the child has developed them they are never forgotten. They keep appearing as his art develops.

Immediately upon the heels of the placement stage come the two shape stages. During the first, the implied shape stage, the child scribbles on his paper with multiple strokes of his crayon. The shape is implied and not contained within a boundary line. But by the age of three he has entered the stage of outline shapes. Now he can outline these implied shapes. He draws circles and ovals, squares and rectangles, triangles, crosses, X's, and a variety of odd but related shapes that only the very young could confidently dream into being.

As soon as children reach the shape stages, they almost immediately move on with a hop, skip, and a short jump to put these shapes into structured forms, like a fat X

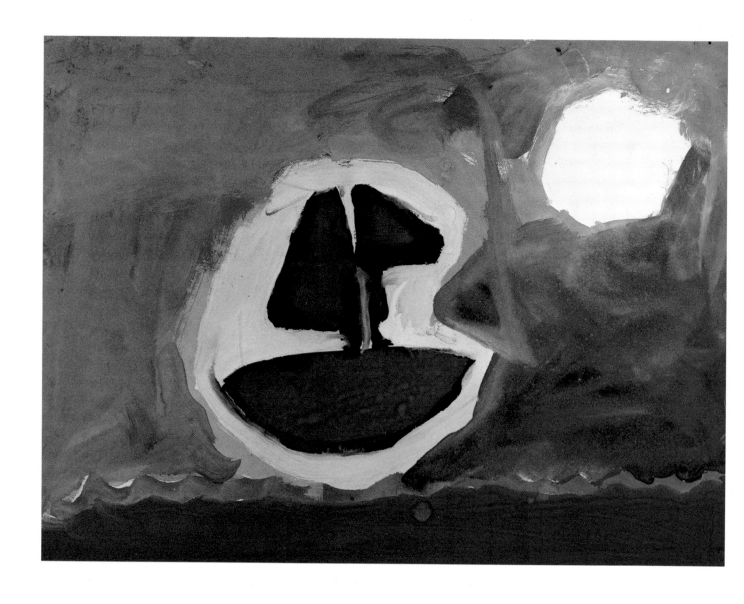

This nimbus-shrouded boat is balanced to sail. That it does not lie upon the sea is a matter of no importance.

inside a square or a thin X and a cross inside a rectangle. Now they are in the design stage.

At last, between the ages of four and five, with a knowledge of the basic scribbles, placement patterns, shapes, and designs stored away and ready to use, children make a dramatic breakthrough. They come to the pictorial stage of their development where, wonderfully, their structured designs begin to look like something that adults have seen before.

This stage may be divided into two parts: early pictorial and later pictorial. The early drawings simply suggest human figures, animals, houses, trees, and the like. The later drawings, however, are clearly defined and easily recognized by adults as familiar objects. They are not more advanced, necessarily. They are just pictures which adults approve of because they are able to recognize them.

In his early pictorial work, the child is seldom concerned with drawing things as they are so much as he is with creating structures that please him. For example, a scribble with many loops serpentining around a house-like shape might look like chimney smoke to an enterprising adult; not so to the child. It's not smoke at all, just a decorative wiggly line that serves to float a figure in the air.

The child's first drawings of the human figure look very strange to adults, for the body is usually round like a ball and the arms sprout jauntily from the head. When he draws these merry creations he does not care whether his pictures look like people. In fact, maybe they are animals; at least adults might call them that because sometimes the ears are placed on top of the head. The same reasoning holds for the buildings which children draw; they may not be houses at all, only variations on designs made up of squares and rectangles. The

Windows on the roof, a dog on the wall, and a torch-like tree make an improbable but happy combination.

child is not drawing objects in the world as he sees them, rather he is striving for something new within a set of forms which he already has learned.

The child's idea of art collides head-on with the typical formulas adults have passed down from one generation to another. Watchful and well-meaning teachers who coax young children to draw real-life objects are not being helpful; indeed, their efforts may stifle the pride, the pleasure, the confidence so necessary to the growth of a creative spirit.

Children who are left alone to draw what they like develop a store of knowledge which enables them to reach their final stage of self-taught art. From that point they may develop into gifted artists, unspoiled. Most children, however, lose interest in drawing after the first few years of school because they are not given this chance to develop freely.

From the bare and beautiful bones of children's art, a skeleton shape has been assembled. Although the search must continue and the message it has for us is yet to be wholly deciphered, part of it is very clear. Its spirit is in the young man on the last page of this book. We see him astride a burro or a horse; for all one can tell, it might be a llama, a yak, or even a saber-toothed tiger. It does not matter. What does matter is that he rides straight in the saddle toward a sun which is rising upon a new day.

2 | Scribbles and Scribbling

Ages 2-3

In the two-year-old's scribbling, there is definite feeling for pattern. Seventeen scribble placement patterns have been identified.

Scribbles are the building blocks of children's art. From the moment the child discovers what it looks like and feels like to put these lines down on paper, he has found something he will never lose, he has found art. This wonderful thing happens to every child when he is about two years old.

The great child psychologist, Arnold Gesell, once said that our knowledge of the child is about as reliable as a 15th Century map of the world. The scribblings of children can help adults find a more reliable map.

At first glance, scribbles may look like tangles of spaghetti, lines without form or distinction.

Actually, there are many kinds of scribbles, some of them are most complex and none of them are senseless. There are some twenty basic scribbles made up of lines that are vertical, horizontal, diagonal, circular, curving,

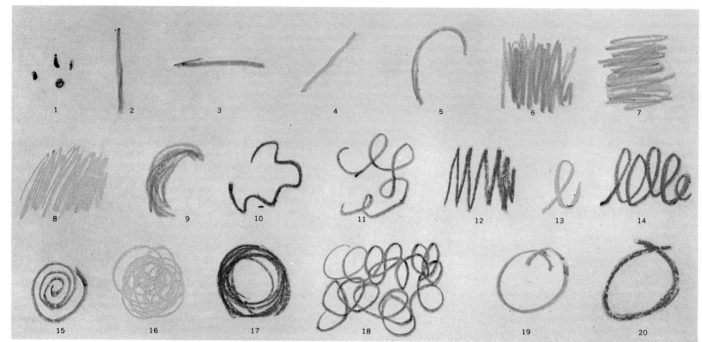

Chart compiled from typical scribbles

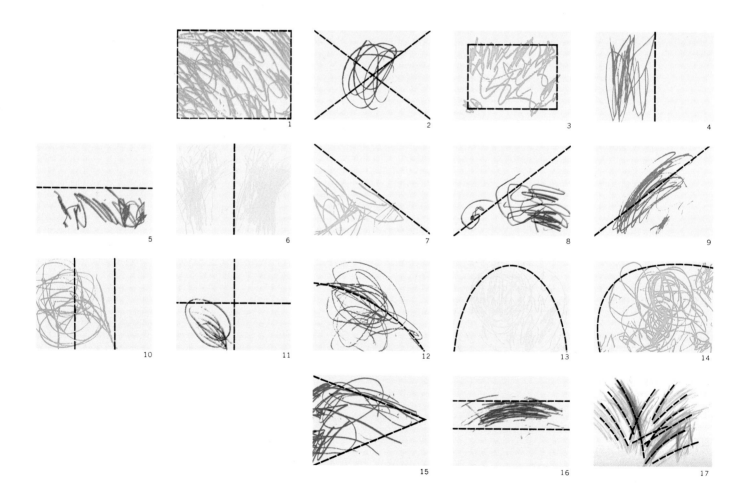

All children use the twenty basic scribbles and scrawl happily with lines that are vertical, horizontal, diagonal, circular, curved, and waving. Scribbles also include patterns of dots.

These are the placement patterns which can be recognized in children's scribbling:

1. overall, the whole page is covered;
2. centered, large or small, but in the middle;
3. spaced border, with page edges clear like a border;
4. and 5. vertical and horizontal halves, only that portion of paper used;
6. two-sided balance, two scribbles balance each other;
7. diagonal half, as though scribbling a triangle;
8. extended diagonal, which spills to the other half-page;
9. diagonal axis, an evenly distributed scribble;
10. two-thirds division, distinctly separated scribbles;
11. quarter-page, with the page thus divided by four;
12. one-corner fan, a flare which leaves three corners empty;
13. two-corner arch, a bridge from page edge to page edge;
14. three-corner arc, only one corner of the page unmarked;
15. two-corner pyramid, two corners are vacant;
16. across the page, like a band or a stripe;
17. base-line fan, using the bottom of the page.

and waving. Scribbles even include patterns of dots.

Scribbling is spontaneous, but the very young child has a feeling for the pattern his markings make against a background. It is almost as though he has an awareness of figure-ground relationship. Seventeen major placement patterns have been identified, and children have their favorites.

One of the scribbles children like best ranges over the paper loosely on a diagonal axis, leaving two corners filled and two corners empty. Scribbling which looks like an arch is just as popular, and still another favorite is the one in which children use up two-thirds of the paper and leave the other one-third blank.

Some parents save their children's pictorial drawings, but few save their children's scribblings. It is difficult for adults to see anything special in the scribbling which every child does in the same way. Certainly it is even harder to see that scribbling is basic to understanding all forms of graphic art. Scribbling is spontaneous, it just happens, and every line in graphic art is built upon it.

When he is a little older, the child will use his scribbles to make hair for people, leaves for trees, smoke for chimneys, and clouds for the skies. But now, as he scribbles, the movement of his hand and arm and body is satisfying. He looks at what he has done and feels a warm glow of creation. Only a short time ago the paper was blank, and now in front of him is something that he alone has made, something that did not exist in the world before.

As a child, Eve may have drawn scribbles in the sands of Eden. If she did, then they looked very much like the scribbles in this section. For children since our first beginnings have drawn in this fashion.

3 | The Secrets of Shape

Ages 2-4

The two-year-old artist discovers shapes hidden within his scribbles. An adult can see these implied shapes, too, if he looks beyond the obvious crayon stroke. There is a triangle hidden here.

A two-year-old could not draw a perfect circle, not with all the wishes and will in the world. He could clutch his crayon bravely, but his coordination would betray his imagination, if, indeed, circles were what he had in mind at all.

But he is in the business of scribbling. And the circles and squares, the rectangles and crosses which he will be drawing so soon and so proudly, now are hidden within the myriad of placement patterns on his paper. They are implied shapes, for scribbling has real form and the very beginnings of shape.

Scribbles know no boundaries. They may fill an entire page—or even part of the tabletop around the page. All the placement patterns appear in the drawings of children by the time they reach the age of three. These patterns are basic, and they are never forgotten.

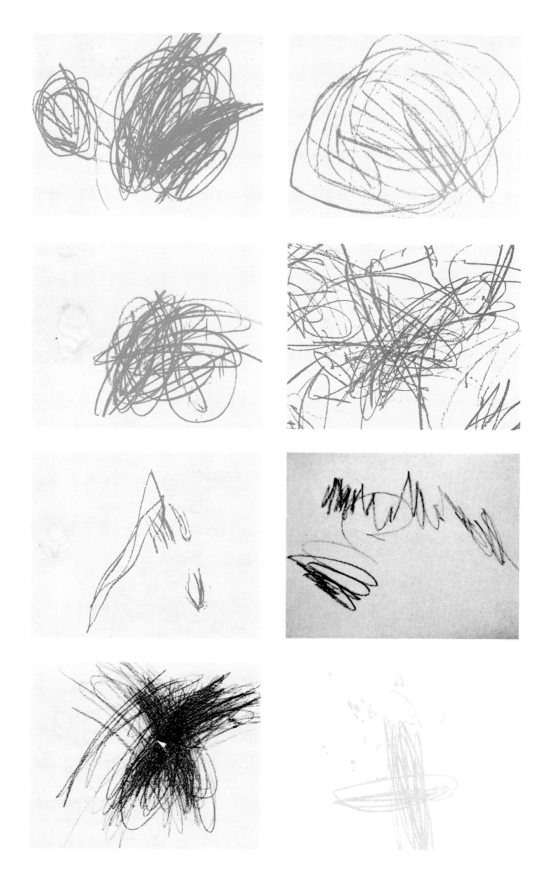

These are the shapes implied in the early scribbling of childhood. They are visible in the samples: circles and ovals, squares and rectangles, triangles, odd shapes, X's, and crosses.

Yet the relationship of the scribbles to the page is only one aspect to consider in children's art. There are hidden shapes for the child to discover and delight in. An adult can see these implied shapes, too, if he lets himself see beauty—not just multiple strokes of a crayon on a page, or what he is accustomed to think of as meaningless pencil scrawls.

Sometimes the child scribbles continuously until the shape is finished. At other times he stops and adds new marks to fill out the whole. Long before the child can draw a square, a circle, or any other shape in outline form, these shapes are implied in his scribbling.

As he starts to scribble, he feels the many possibilities that lie before him. He can scribble this way or that, or some other way entirely, just as he pleases. And once he has begun to scribble he can change his mind, which he often does.

This is the feeling of children in their twos. The two-year-old doesn't start out with a plan in mind, but when he looks at a scribble after it is finished, he sees a visual whole, an entity. The child's view is illustrated perfectly in the answer of a little nursery-school girl whose foolish teacher asked, "What are you drawing?" The child explained it all, "How do I know until I have finished?"

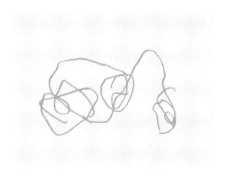

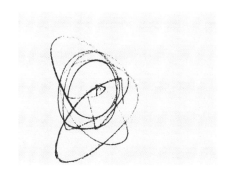

Recipe for finger paintings like the ones
on these two pages and the next: Take two cups of flour and
five cups of cold water and cook until smooth.
Add some salt and let it cool. Next comes the baker's food dye,
and the paint's ready. Then give the child a smock
made of Dad's castoff shirt, turn him loose, and stand far back.

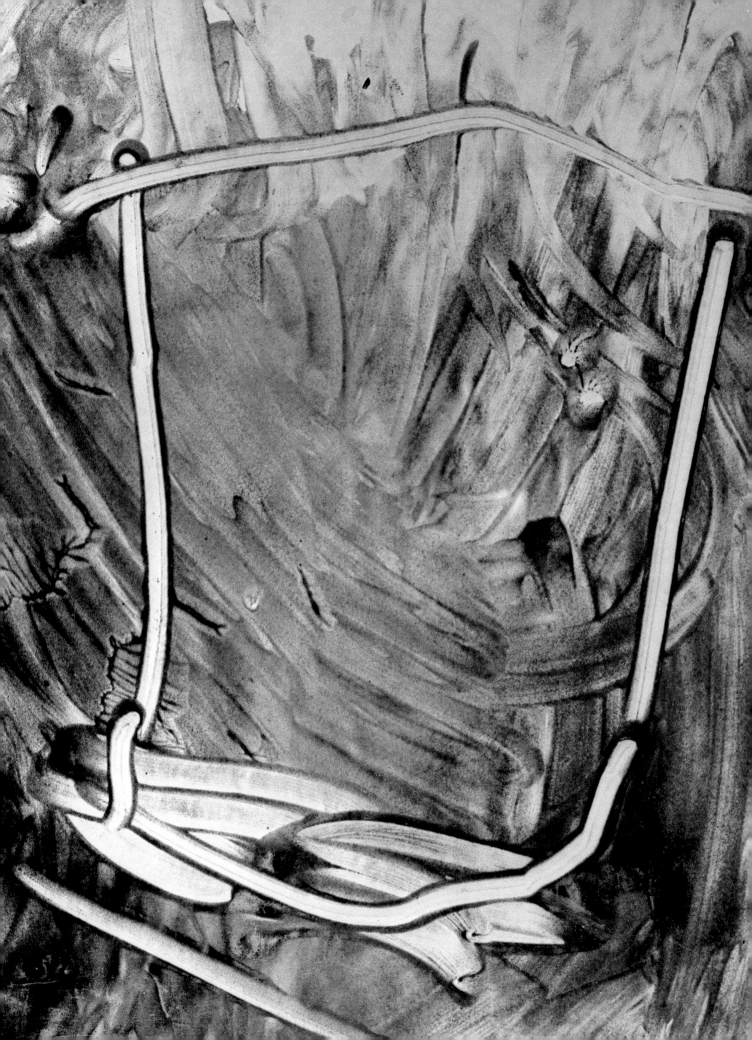

4 | Art In Outline

Ages 3-4

As soon as the child can outline the forms he sees in his scribbles, he moves quickly forward in his development. This rectangle within a finger painting represents a moment of discovery for a three-year-old. He has found a building block essential for creating designs.

And then there is a very special day for every child when he is about three. He grasps his crayon firmly, and with a single line he draws a form he likes in his scribbles, and then another and still another. He can outline shapes.

He may be tentative at first in this new work. But not for long. He remembers the implied shapes in his earlier scribblings and he draws them in outline. His circles may look like Dali-esque watches, limp and droopy, but they are round.

He draws some shapes which defy classification. And he draws circles and ovals, triangles, rectangles, and squares, clean crosses, and exuberant X's. At least those are the shapes that adults see, but they should remember that through years of living they have accumulated a store of rich associations

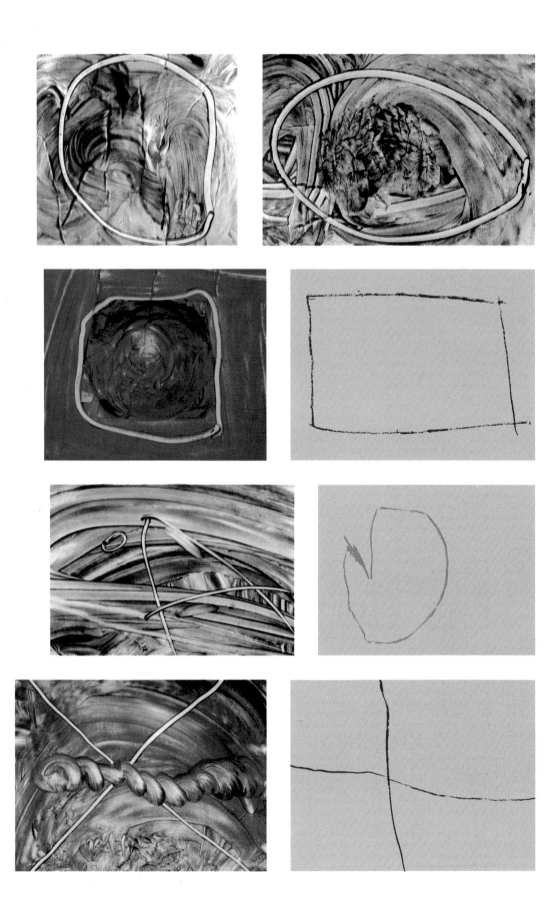

Now the child has found that he can outline every conceivable shape he needs in his later art work. The circles and ovals, squares and rectangles, triangles, odd shapes, X's and crosses are clearly recognizable now to adults, as well as to children.

which children have yet to acquire. Thus, to an adult a big round O may be a letter in the alphabet, a circle, an ornament, a ring, or perhaps even a wheel. To the child it is only a pleasing shape, nothing more. And this is not the time to push the child along by imposing adult definitions, it is a time to let his self-taught art develop. This advice is not always easy to follow. A child may scribble all over his paper, then proudly hold it up to his nursery-school teacher and say, "That is my daddy's car."

Well, it is not a picture of daddy's car nor grandma's car nor anyone's car. It is a shape, and the teacher who really wishes to be helpful can say that the drawing has nice lines in it, that it has pretty triangles, or something else true and encouraging.

Most adults rate a child's drawing according to how well it represents a person or a house, a boat, a tree, or any familiar object at all. Such a strict representational approach all too often robs the adult of appreciating the wealth of structured, nonpictorial work which children teach themselves before they pictorialize.

This is a very important time and a satisfying one for every two- and three-year-old as he grows in art. Michelangelo, looking up in contemplation at the finished ceiling of the Sistine Chapel, may never have felt more pride than does the child when, wonderingly, he gazes upon his own first circular outline.

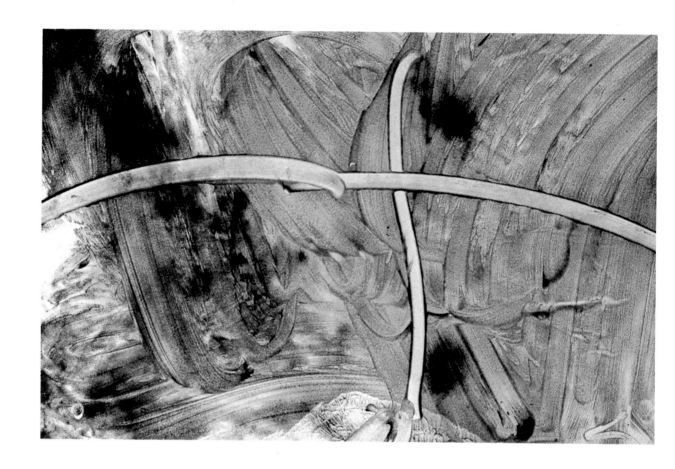

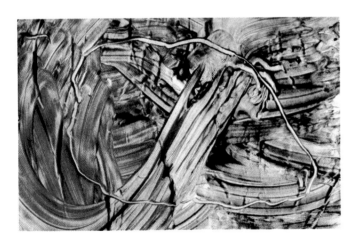

A few of the various steps of creative art are shown in the picture at the top of the page.
Somber-hued strokes of the palm or the side of a hand provide the base. A moment's pause while the artist
surveys the creation, his full weight on his hands, is followed by delicate, one-finger tracings.

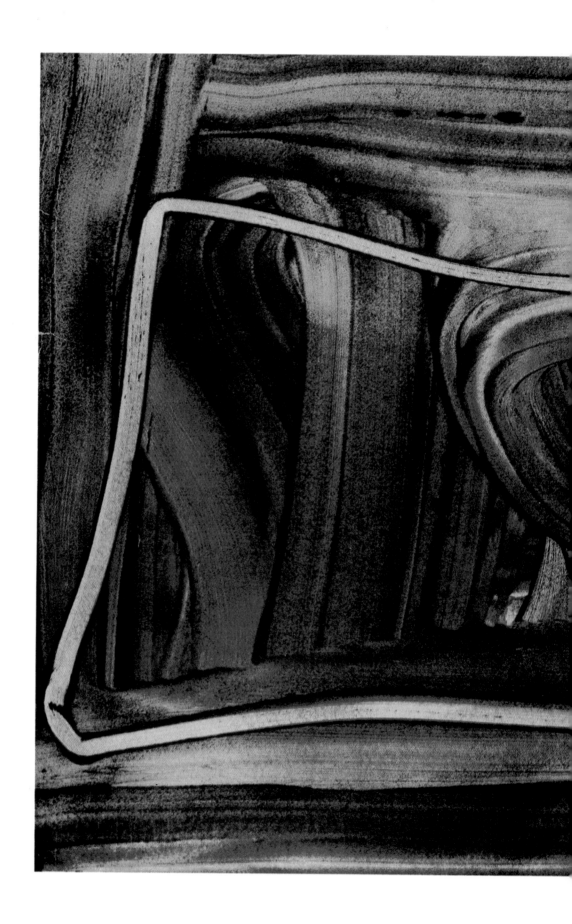

5 | The Child and Design

Ages 3-5

When the three-year-old discovers he can make designs, he draws confidently, and with real flourish. This design has everything—circles, squares, triangles, crosses, and shapes that defy classification.

Almost from the moment they are able to draw shapes in outline form, children begin to combine these forms into designs. In the beginning their designs are simple.

A circle may be placed inside a square, or maybe it looks just as nice the other way around to a child and so he puts the square inside the circle. To go a step further, he may add a cross inside of both of them for balance and for fun. And all at once his design becomes far more complex and interesting.

Seeking variety within a set of forms already learned, the child soon begins to put many shapes together in an altogether pleasing fashion.

When a child can put two outlined shapes together into a design, his horizons expand dramatically, for among his remembered shapes are many possible

The wonderful design combinations are all here, clearly. There are circles within an oval, rectangles combined with circles, squares within circles, triangles combined with circles, a double triangle, a marvelously odd shape surrounding a rectangle, and a complex X plus cross design.

combinations. If he uses more than two shapes, the combinations become virtually unlimited. Usually, however, children draw only a few favorites.

Designs in which shapes stand out in a balanced relationship tend to dominate children's art. As children draw designs they arrange them on their paper in the familiar placement patterns.

As the three-year-old struggles to express his new ideas, the lines he draws are sometimes faint and often unsure. But once the outline shapes become familiar to him, he puts them down with strength and with a very real flourish.

Children develop a style of their own which teachers and parents can recognize easily. But up to and including the age of five, children's drawings are very much alike. Even the drawings of boys cannot be told from those of girls.

For both boys and girls, three is a confident age in the development of their art. They know what they are doing, as surely as the little girl who, when asked to explain her drawing, answered, "This is not a story...it's a picture to look at."

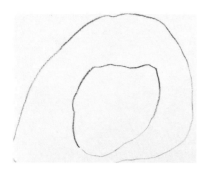

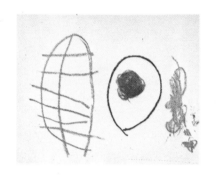

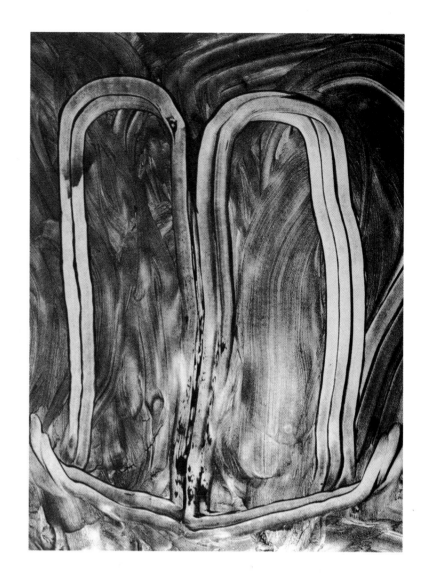

46

The picture shown above may look to an adult like a golden ladder rising between the blue waters of a sea and the red sands of a desert. But to the child who traced the ladder with the tips of four small fingers and made the sea with a swirl of his palm, it is just a design.

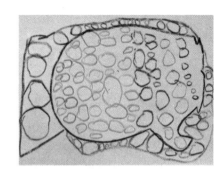

Are the two large pictures eyeball-to-eyeball confrontations? How many circles can be placed within a circle or around the edge of a rectangle? And how do squares and rectangles grow in Mary's garden of outline shapes? Fascination with the newly acquired ability to control a crayon or brush proliferates an unending array of shape and line.

6 | Mandalas, Suns, and Radials

Ages 3-5

The mandala, a simple crossed circle, has always been one of man's favorite compositions. This is the finger painting of a three-year-old.

Mandalas have been used by the human race for countless centuries. They have been carved upon stones of the jungle and the walls of prehistoric caves, scratched upon pottery and painted upon the facades of elaborate temples. They are among the oldest magical and religious symbols known to mankind. Modern children draw them too, beginning at the age of three.

Mandala is a Sanskrit word and means a "magic circle," though crossed squares and concentric circles and squares also count as mandalas.

The distinguishing feature of a mandala, besides the romantic sound of the word, is its perfect balance. Mandalas are designs that challenge perfection because symmetry has no end and infinity is beautiful. In the self-taught art of the child, including his earliest

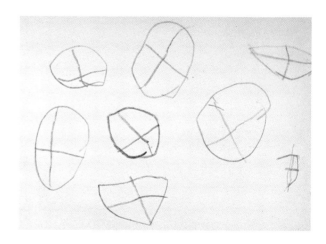

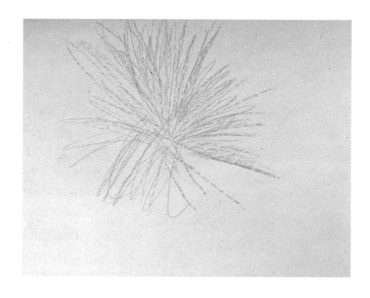

These are examples of mandalas, suns, and radials. In a mandala, a large area is divided into even parts; in a sun, radiating lines touch or cross the outlined shape; in a radial, lines radiate from a central point.

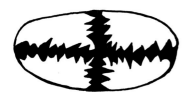

Paleolithic man liked to make mandalas, too. These tracings are from pebbles now in the Museum of St. Germain, in France. They were painted more than 3000 years ago.

abstractions and the later pictorial drawings, mandala balance is a favorite.

Mandalas are an important point of departure from which the child proceeds to draw suns, radials, and, eventually, human figures.

In its most simple form of a circle crossed by lines, the mandala suggests the sun. But it is only a suggestion. The child draws a circular shape and crosses his circle with interesting lines, in precisely the way the "design" has been drawn since the earliest days of mankind. In children's art, the center markings soon disappear, the lines cross only the outside of the shape, and the real sun emerges. At a later stage, children may add various scribbles to the suns to make humans, animals, flowers, and other objects.

After the child draws suns, he begins to experiment further and starts to draw a series of lines which spray out from a point or from a very small area like a circle. These line drawings are called radials, and add strength and vitality to the child's designs. Later, they will become spokes in a wheel, whiskers on a cat, and fireworks in the sky.

When the child makes a sun form and radials, his parents and teachers may rightly feel that he has taken a giant step forward and is on the path to many other exciting things.

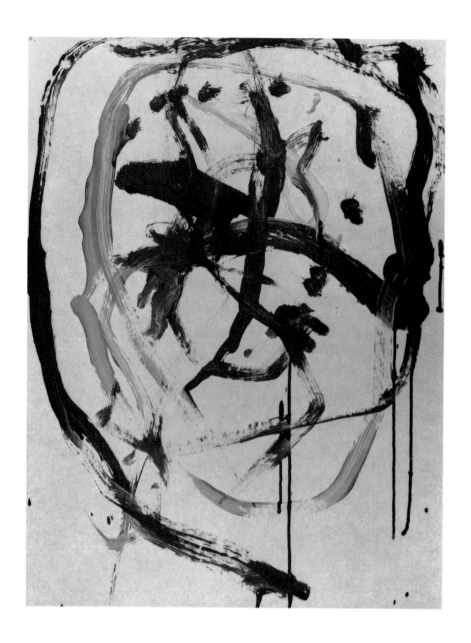

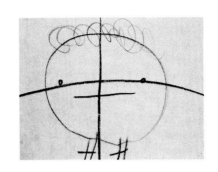

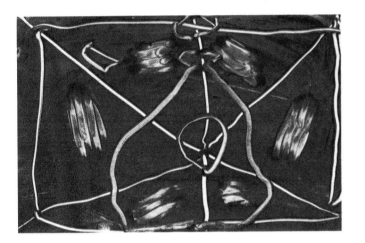
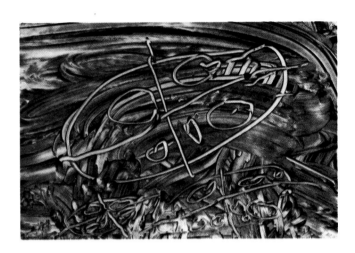

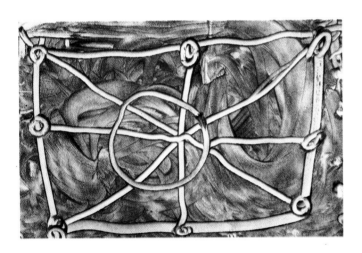

The large painting on the opposite page accidentally conceals within a basic mandala an outline of a human face. The crayon drawing, below on the opposite page, with its rim of flower petals and a flower person in each quarter, is an advanced mandala.

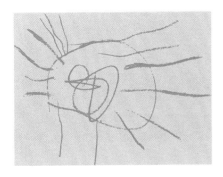

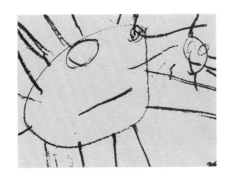

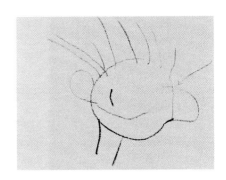

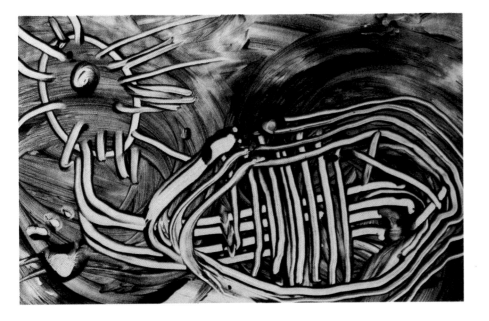

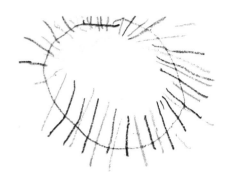

The sun symbol is repeated in all of these pictures—though some are faces, some are purely decoration, and some could be big fat spiders lying in wait for Little Miss Muffit.

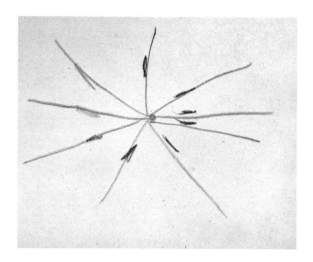

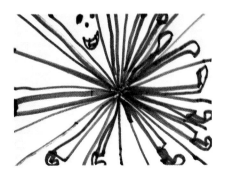
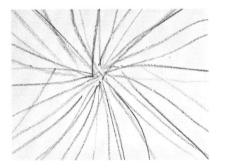

Radials can be common asterisks, plants with waving fronds,
Fourth of July explosions, Christmas stars, a happy pinwheel of arms
and legs and a smiling face, or if the center of the radial
is expanded, a familiar sun.

7 | People, People, People

Ages 4-5

This is a mandala-type human.
The parts are arranged to fit beautifully
into a circle. The lines at the top right
of the painting complete the circle,
not the human.

The favorite subject of people is people. And so it is with children and their art. As soon as they are able, at about the age of four, children begin to draw the human figure.

Interestingly, this follows in art soon after the child can make mandalas and draw the sun which shines so brightly in his work and on his days. From the sun in his drawings comes the human face, at first huge in its relationship to arms and legs.

The first people drawings naturally seem pretty inhuman. Rays of the sun become arms and legs, ears, hair, and head decorations. A child may take away some of the sun's rays and lengthen others, add scribbles for facial features, use small suns for hands and rays for fingers. In the first drawings of humans, the arms are attached to the head, and there are markings on

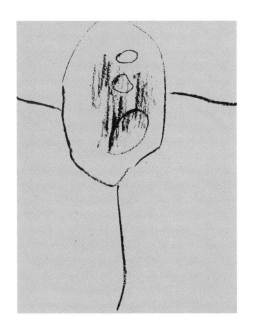 

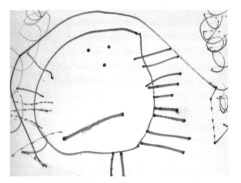  

There is charm in a child's early humans. Whatever his treatment of arms and legs and faces, the total effect is always pleasing.

top—not for hair, really, but to balance the legs. In later drawings, the child omits arms, perhaps in an effort to relieve the monotony of mandala balance.

For each child is striving always for balance, design, and variety within a set of self-taught esthetic formulas. Most of the drawings of humans done before the age of six are made to fit into an implied circle or one of its variations, no matter what distortions of anatomy may be required. It is important to remember that at this stage the child is not trying to draw a human likeness but only to place things in a way that looks right and is pleasing to him.

These mandala-inspired figures, by the very nature of their form, arrange themselves comfortably within a crossed circle. In a child's drawing of the human figure, the head and arms and legs often fall into balance on the lines of this cross. If the cross is diagonal, then the figure that follows its lines may be thought of by adults as a dancer, or as someone in distress who seems to be calling for help.

As long as children feel free to draw naturally, balance remains a prominent feature of their work. They are especially concerned with adding balance to the tops of their people. They do this by drawing most amazing ears and lots of hair, but particularly by adding hats, hats in every form and size, hats by the millions.

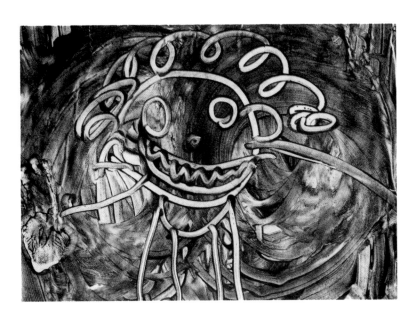

Evolving suns drowned in galactic clouds spin off eyes that stare from early human faces. Arms reach out to keep a delicate balance and circles float in eerie processions when children begin to draw the people they see about them.

Children love to draw hats. Boys draw them as often as girls do, but the hats on boys tend to be simpler in style than those on girls, though few are so wildly ornate as the one on the opposite page, with its trailing draperies, feathery plumes, and jeweled crown.

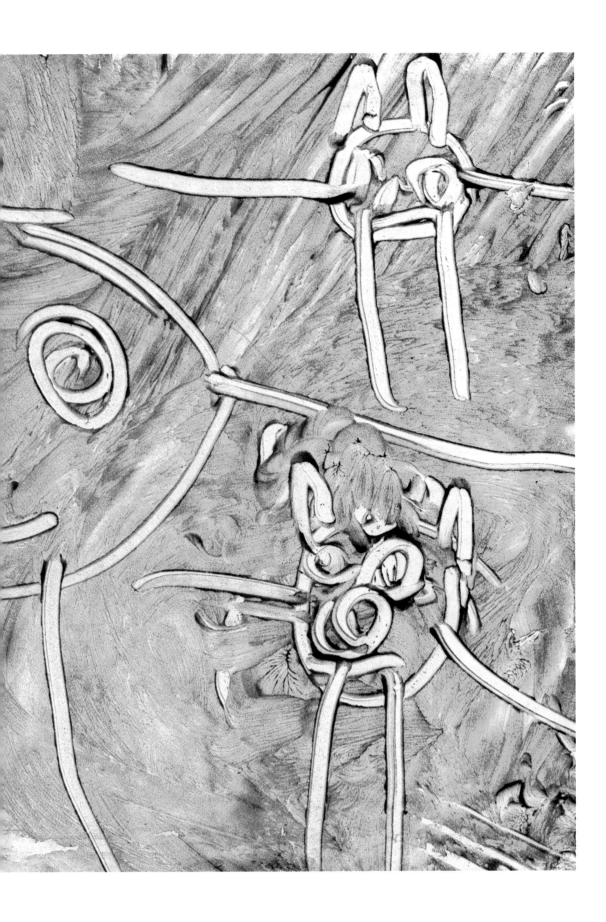

8 | Almost Pictures

Ages 4-6

In his early pictorial work, the child is just beginning to paint and draw animals. He also tries buildings, trees, flowers, boats, cars and airplanes. In child art, humans become animals when there are ears on top of the head instead of hats or hair.

Between the ages of four and five, most children arrive at the pictorial stage in the development of their art. Their drawings of people are the first clear sign, and then their designs begin to look like objects which adults may recognize.

The child's drawings of the human figure are followed after a while by pictures of animals which stand up firmly on two legs instead of crouching down on all fours. The child simply puts two ears on top of a head he has drawn, and he has something which adults obligingly call an animal. Very often he draws two arms, or sometimes three or four, on one side of the figure, and then the drawing looks like any number of exotic creatures.

The child's first stark picture of a tree looks quite like an armless human. Later trees have markings that are meant to be fruit or blossoms—the familiar sun he

In early pictures, animals are modified humans; houses are special combinations of squares and rectangles; flowers are circles on a stem; airplanes are basically diagonal cross designs; and automobiles are houses on wheels.

has been drawing becomes a flower perched on bushy leaves, and the shapes he has been using for hair now represent petals. He is making almost pictures because his work essentially is still design.

Children use the same simple formulas to make creatures they haven't seen and boats they haven't sailed. A triangle surmounting a square is called a boat. A rectangle or a square balanced atop two circles is called a car or a wagon. In each case, the label usually has been applied by an eager or imaginative adult. In the same way, the first buildings which children conjure up so whimsically are not meant to be real houses at all, just a design of squares and rectangles.

Left to themselves, children will draw representationally when they are ready. They will want to picture something from their own lives, from stories read to them or from their own fantasy world. They will do this in their own good time without adult interpretation.

Children of the world, wherever they live, make all their early drawings—humans and houses, trees and boats— in the same way. They are building upon the creative impulse which is the heritage of all mankind and is limited to no one land or culture. A Glasgow girl, for example, can walk into the house of a girl in San Francisco and see the same things she has been drawing at home in Scotland.

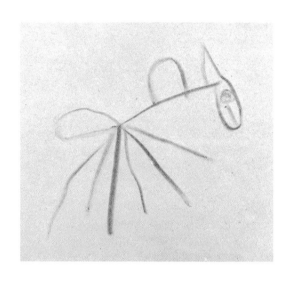

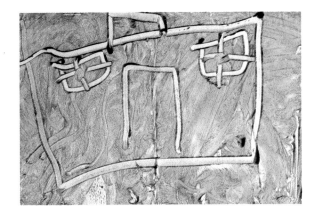
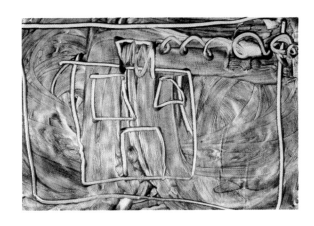

Houses are human. Some are glum and others are gay. Still others are simply bewildered. Animals can be human too. They come with human faces, feet, and hair, with two human legs or a dozen, and their offspring always run true to the breed.

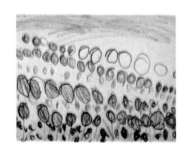

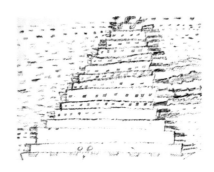

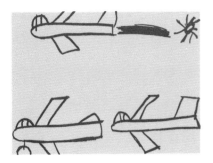

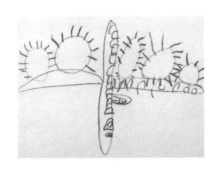

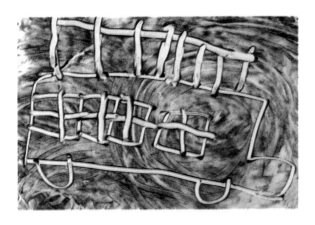

Grandfather would have felt right at home in any of these high-behind, big-wheeled automobiles (Henry Ford's first scribble?) which are produced from the archetypal forms of rectangles, squares, and circles on the child's assembly line.

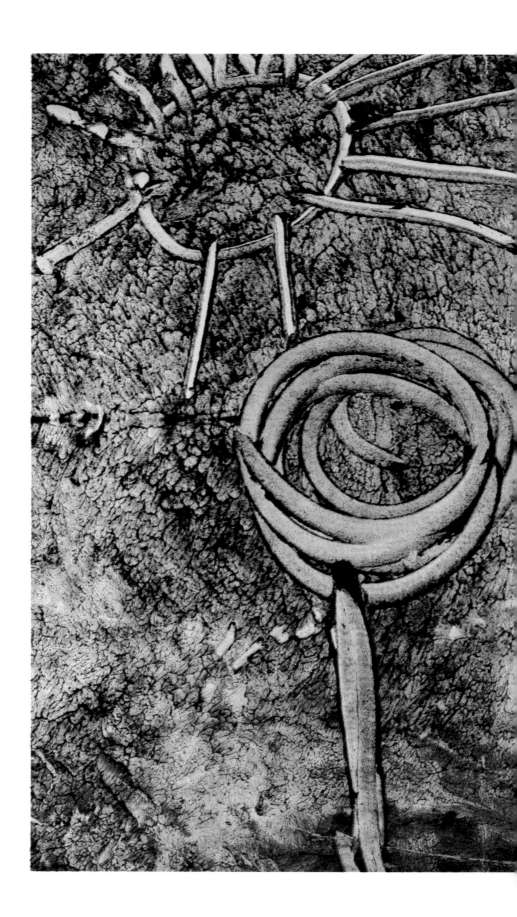

9 | Pictures

Ages 5-7

The critical period in child art is between the ages of five and seven. The child who feels free to use the colors and basic shapes which please him will continue to flourish artistically when he moves into pictorial work.

In his early pictorial work, a child paints or draws one person or many people, one house or many houses, but they are still designs. Not until he is five or six years old do his pictures begin to tell their own story.

Then he will put children, kites, houses, the sun, and the sky into one drawing. He will paint houses on hills and animals in farmyards. Where he has been thinking in terms of individual objects, he now puts a collection of objects in his work.

From his first pictorial drawings in which trees often look like people, eyes are but simple dots, ears are difficult to tell from arms, and animals have more legs than any animal needs, the child moves next into a world of art to which adults can relate better.

This new world, however, still is the child's own. He brings to it art forms which he himself has developed

Four suns, drooping smoke, and exaggerated rainbows may be necessary to give balance to children's compositions. The first four drawings on the opposite page have in common the remarkable sense of spacing which is natural to children.

out of his memory. He also brings to it new physical strength and coordination. He can use almost any art media now, and he can even handle paintbrushes well. Though he suddenly seems far more advanced in his art, a good part of this apparent leap forward is just plain increased dexterity. He can control his crayon better and bear down harder or draw more lightly than before. If he wants to color within an outline, he can stay inside the boundaries he set with his paints and crayons.

To most people, child art calls to mind the stick figures which children draw as representations of people. Actually, the stick figure is not a spontaneous product of child art. It is a figure children learn after the age of five from adults or from other children whose parents or teachers already have shown them this particular formula for a person.

There is a tremendous creative impulse both in the child who eventually will become a great artist and in the child who will be a businessman, or the mother of artists and businessmen. Too often, children lose interest in art at about the age of seven because they feel the disapproval of adults who try to prod them into neat and acceptable art molds.

The little girl who went to the park for a drawing lesson and drew a tree with a red trunk and blue leaves is a good example of how too many children are nudged away from art. When her grade-school teacher asked the supervisor what could possibly be done with such a child, and though great artists have painted blue leaves and great writers have described them as such, the supervisor said, "Take her back to the park."

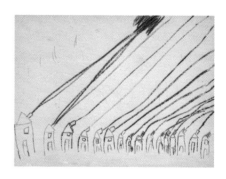

The drawing at the upper right of the hungry cowboys home from the round-up shows perfect balance if not perfect etiquette. And what could be more balanced than the pictures of houses frolicking around in logical disorder!

10 | Hidden Treasures

Art does not have to be pictorial
to be pleasing. In this pastel simple
color and line arrest the eye.

Once upon a time, the best a primary school could offer in the way of art was the stiff outline of a carrot or a Santa Claus in faded purple ink to be filled in by colored crayons.

Now that Kandinsky and Klee, Chagall, Picasso, and Miro have returned to the sources of child art and manipulated these shapes and patterns in sophisticated ways, the creations of the young receive some of the attention they deserve. Scribblings that once were thrown into the wastebasket are looked at with respect and even pleasure by those who have become sympathetic to the aims and needs of the child.

Aware that art need not be representational to be esthetically rewarding, many adults have learned to like scribblings for their shapes, colors, and balance. But as children move on to the pictorial stage and begin to mix pictorial and nonpictorial elements in their work, the usual

Design, not subject matter, determines the minor features of children's work. Details needed for balance may not be attractive to adults.

reaction is to wait, patiently or not, until the child discovers how to draw properly.

Yet it is not hard to appreciate the art of early childhood. It is only necessary to know that there is in children's art no intent to create a picture in the adult sense of the word. To find a crooked house, on a crooked street, should not cause alarm. The house stands askew, inviting the rain, just as a matter of simple design.

It helps to remember that everything the child discovers in art he appropriates and uses again and again. And so a small circle inscribed with a cross may casually blossom one day as a flower in the grass. It may also appear in the very same picture as a button on a dress or, because the child is pleased by the pattern, in the form of a harvest sun.

Much has been learned about children's scribblings, but there is much that is still unknown. The hidden message, when fully deciphered, will enable the viewer to recapture the un-*adult*-erated vision of the child.

Perhaps the day will come when adult and child can enjoy self-taught art together, not as cute or remarkable products of the childish mind but as the groundwork of all art. Then adults will not make stencils for children to fill in, nor will they laugh at what they do not understand.

Who is so unfortunate that he has never seen such things as a pink ship afloat upon a ghostly sea, nor a little girl at the wheel of a scoop machine, nor an evening sun encircled by a skyrocket of birds and butterflies?

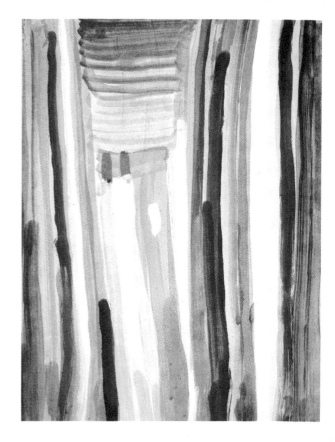

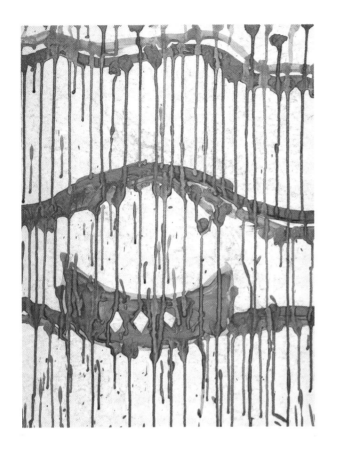

Looking at these pictures of never-never land, where trees grow like turnips, and rainbows are square, and water falls up instead of down, calls to mind a remark made long ago which likened the taste of mango fruit to a stroll through a jungle at midnight while eating a dish of ice cream.

11 | Around the World

This picture of fun on a merry-go-round might have been painted by any child in any country. It is the work of a Chinese girl of six who lives in San Francisco.

Prehistoric man carved upon the walls of his cave, using stone tools, simple markings that children of today in nursery school repeat upon paper with crayon and pencil and their fingers.

The little girl from Glasgow and the girl from Chattanooga draw houses that look alike. The Tibetan boy draws a tiger that looks like a donkey or a cow or a buffalo or all these animals at once, and it might easily be the work of a boy who lives in New York.

A medicine man with a string of human bones around his neck, in a lost jungle of the Congo, draws a crossed circle upon a rock to propitiate the gods and invoke rain. At the same moment, halfway around the world, a child in a starched dress with a pink ribbon in her hair stands before an easel and paints, only to please herself, the same crossed circle.

103

Ceylon

United States

India

Indonesia

Bali

Switzerland

These pictures were drawn by children from different lands, but their intricate details have much in common.

These many expressions of art prove two significant things.

Cultures the world over, however simple or advanced, use the same forms to express what they wish to say. The forms may appear to change from one country to another, but at heart they remain alike.

The art of young children everywhere is identical. It comes from the same beginnings and uses the same shapes found in primitive art. The walls of tombs and the shards of ancient pottery and the finger paintings of today's child each bear the same testimony — that in art all mankind is one.

Not until the weight of culture lays a burden upon the child can the art of one country and century be told from that of another. The child then assumes the style of his own time and place.

Even after our culture has imposed its mark upon the artist there is no need of an interpreter. The wooden mask from Africa and the antique horse carved from stone centuries ago in China and the watercolor painted by the brush of a living artist may be found in the house of today. They look well together. They speak the language of esthetics, which is understood by all cultures in all ages.

The magic is that children in each new generation use this language from the day they make their first scribble on paper or patterns in the sand or circles in the air.

Italy

Greece

Thailand

Iran

India

Ceylon

Greece

Hong Kong

Egypt

Universality of art among the world's young children is demonstrated by the drawings in this section. If children everywhere are so much alike that they use identical shapes, designs, and symbols, then it may be possible to build upon man's common heritage rather than to founder upon his differences.

Holland

Spain

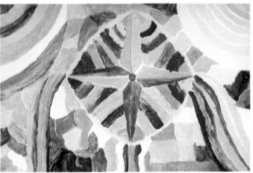

Philippines

Taiwan

Taiwan

108

Finland

Israel

Here are two pictures from
Taiwan, another picture from
Holland, and others from the
Philippines, Finland, Israel,
and Spain. Without a clue it
would be hard to recognize the
native country of these child artists.
For neither the location nor the
era changes the common heritage
of all mankind.

Illustrations

Illustrations are listed as they appear when read from left to right, top to bottom. Ages are listed in years, plus months. Sizes of original art in inches.

*unknown

Book design by Tom Suzuki